# PRESERVED
# STEAM TRAINS
## OF
# BRITAIN

# PRESERVED
# STEAM TRAINS
## OF
# BRITAIN

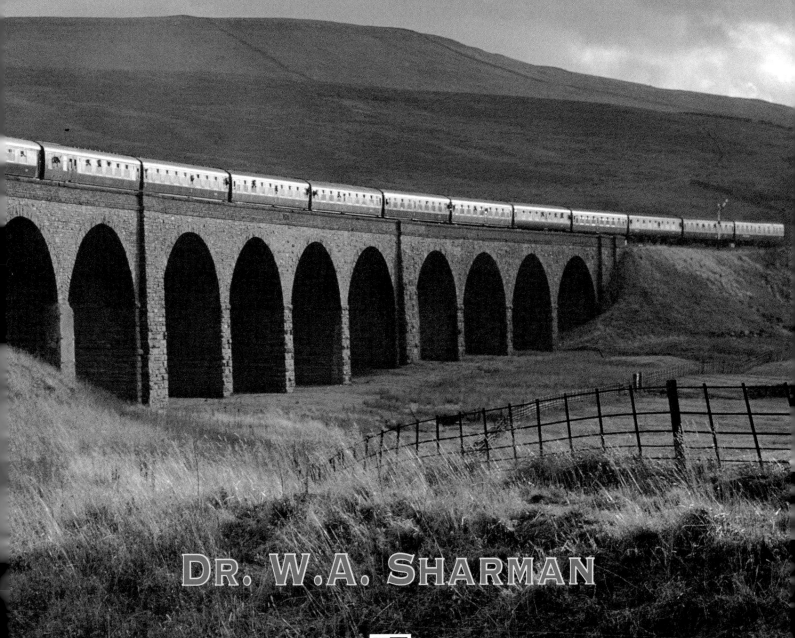

# DR. W.A. SHARMAN

MILEPOST

Milepost 92¹/₂
Newton Harcourt
Leicestershire
LE8 9FH
Tel 0116 2592068

MILEPOST

◀ **(Page 1)** 71000 "Duke of Gloucester" was the prototype of a new Standard Class 8 Pacific locomotive. Built in 1954, it was the only engine in its class. On a lovely summers day it leaves Birkett Tunnel with a southbound "Cumbrian Mountain Express"

◀ **(Pages 2-3)** Ex LMS "Coronation" class No. 46229 "Duchess of Hamilton" - the flagship of the National Railway Museum's collection - catches the last rays of the setting winter sun whilst leaving Garsdale over Dandry Mire viaduct with a northbound "Cumbrian Mountain Express"

▶ **(Opposite)** Ex LMS "Jubilee" class No. 5690 "Leander" passes Lostock Gralam signal box en-route from Northwich to Leeds with a "Trans-Pennine Pullman". This locomotive was withdrawn from BR service in March 1964 and spent 8 years in Barry scrapyard before being restored to main line condition at Derby in 1972. "Leander" was one of the busiest and most popular locomotives in the early days of preserved steam on the main line.

# INTRODUCTION

The magic of steam is indefinable, and indeed means different things to different people. The steam locomotive is a living thing - it barks and wheezes, shouts and whistles at you - and each engine seems to have it's own personality. When you put this fiery monster into the glorious fells of Cumbria, the wild and rugged grandeur of the "Road to the Isles" or the lush landscape of the "Welsh Marches", then you can understand why photographing steam locomotives becomes an incurable disease.

My own interest in railways began in the late 1940s when our family travelled by train from Manchester to enjoy our annual summer holiday in Brightlingsea in Essex. My memory is one of fast, exciting expresses whisking me from Manchester, through Leicester to London, a trip across London to an atmospheric Liverpool Street station, and then a magical journey to Brightlingsea changing at Colchester and

Wivenhoe. On this latter part of the trip each successive train got smaller and smaller and was hauled by increasingly geriatric engines. At the end of the journey my loco spotting book was red hot!

When the curtain was finally rung down on steam on British Railways on August 11th 1968, and it was decreed that no preserved steam locomotive would be allowed to run over British Rail metals, it seemed to steam enthusiasts that a new "Dark Ages" had arrived. Steam retreated to the confines of a few preserved lines, kept alive by a handful of hard-working and dedicated enthusiasts. Some of these enthusiasts formed the "Return to Steam" committee of the Association of Railway Preservation Societies, and quietly, patiently and diplomatically negotiated with British Rail to effect the return of steam specials to the main line. In October 1971 they were rewarded with an experimental

8 day exhibition tour by 6000 "King George V" hauling 8 coaches. Stop-overs were arranged at various places on the route. The tour was a resounding success, thousands of people flocking to see the train. As a direct consequence, 12 steam hauled trains were sanctioned to run on the main line in 1972, and this was expanded to 18 in 1973. The return of 4472 "Flying Scotsman" from it's stay in America in February 1973 set the seal of success on all the hard work carried out by the enthusiasts up and down the country. In 1973 we would have found it hard to believe that in 1985 some 235 steam hauled excursions would run on British Rail.

Steam on the main line is the icing on the cake. There is nothing to match the awesome power of an express locomotive hauling a heavy train at main line speeds. However, the foundations for this pinnacle of achievement are rooted in the preserved railways, manned, for the most part, by unpaid, dedicated enthusiasts. Many of these

preserved lines have survived only after tackling and overcoming the most fearsome odds with sheer hard work, grit and determination.

The first part of this book, therefore, depicts some of the preserved lines in this country, which are often home to many of the locomotives which appear on the main line. From there we look at a small part of the main line scene. Finally there is a short section showing how the weather and climatic conditions can be harnessed to enhance steam photography.

Steam railway photography is a very personal thing. Let me show you some of the Preserved Steam Locomotives of this country - "As I Saw Them"

W.A.Sharman,
Lyddington,
November 1995

Ex GWR "Castle" class No. 5029 "Nunney Castle" leaves Loughborough with the 15.15 for Leicester North. This locomotive, which is currently a regular performer on the main line, was on loan for a short time to the Great Central Railway from the Great Western Society at Didcot where it is based.

Arguably one of the most scenic of the preserved lines is the North Yorkshire Moors Railway. Certainly the 1 in 49 climb from Grosmont to Goathland is one of the severest sustained gradients on any preserved line. For a short spell in 1984, 62005 appeared in BR black livery, though normally it carries the apple green LNER livery and the number 2005. This picture is taken at Water Ark with the 10.55 departure from Grosmont.

(Over) Ex SR "Merchant Navy" class Bulleid Pacific No 35028 "Clan Line" powers away from Shrewsbury heading south with a "Welsh Marches Express". This locomotive was withdrawn from service in July 1967 from Nine Elms shed on the ending of steam on the Southern Region and was purchased for preservation by the Merchant Navy Society.

◀ A welcome visitor to the Great Central Railway is the Cheddleton Railway Centre's ex LMS "Derby Four" class 4F No. 4422. It is working the 10.45 ex Loughborough to Leicester North service train over the newly laid section of double track at Kinchley Lane.

🔽 Ex SR "West Country" class No. 34039 "Boscastle" was withdrawn from Eastleigh in May 1965 and spent 8 years in Barry scrapyard before moving to the Great Central Railway for restoration. The locomotive is seen at Kinchley Lane working the 14.25 ex Loughborough.

⬥ Another visitor, this time from the Birmingham Railway Museum at Tyseley, is ex LMS "Jubilee" class No. 5593 "Kolhapur" leaving Loughborough with the 10.00 for Leicester North. It appears here in LMS black livery, though in it's time on the railway has appeared in LMS red livery and BR green livery.

⬖ Ex GWR "Modified Hall" class No. 6960 "Ravenham Hall" was built in 1944 - a Hawkesworth improvement to the already successful Collett design. Withdrawn from Oxford shed in June 1964, it spent 9 years in Barry scrapyard before being restored at Steamtown Museum, Carnforth in time for the Rail 150 celebrations at Shildon in 1975. Moved to the Severn Valley Railway in 1977 where it is seen crossing Oldbury viaduct with the 13.05 ex Bridgenorth.

◗ The Severn Valley Railway, running from Bridgenorth to Kidderminster is a delightful example of a branch line with several attractive country stations. Ex LMS 2F class No. 46443 crosses Oldbury viaduct shortly after leaving Bridgenorth.

The Keighley and Worth Valley Railway probably packs more into it's 5 mile run than practically any other railway. Mytholmes viaduct is a well-loved photographic location. Ex SR "USA" Tank No. 30072 and Haydock Foundry 0-6-0WT "Bellerophon" (built 1874) are seen here with a mixed freight.

Mytholmes viaduct as seen from the opposite side with ex LMS class 3F No. 47279 hauling a typical branch line stopping passenger train - the 09.27 from Keighley.

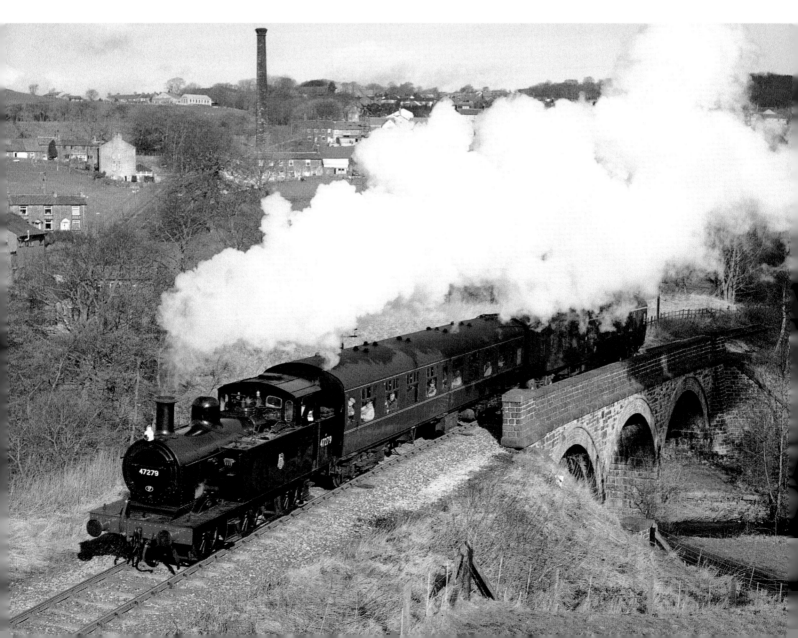

⬆ Visiting engine from the Great Western Society, Didcot ex GWR 2-6-2T No. 6106 leaves Ingrow with the 11.42 ex Keighley.

⬇ Ex BR Standard Class 4 No. 75078 was rescued from Barry scrapyard in 1972 after a 6 year stay, and was subsequently restored at Haworth. In this picture, 75078 and 6106 approaches Oakworth - made famous by the film "The Railway Children" - with the 14.42 ex Keighley.

◀ Ex BR Class 9F No. 92220 "Evening Star" was the last steam locomotive built for British Rail in 1960. A National Railway Museum locomotive, it has appeared extensively on the main line. Here it is leaving Goathland with the 13.55 ex Grosmont for Pickering.

▼ Ex SR "West Country" Class No. 34027 "Taw Valley" is another main line steam engine currently resident on the North Yorkshire Moors Railway. Withdrawn from Salisbury shed in August 1964, it languished in Barry scrapyard until April 1980 when it was purchased and restored to main line running standard. It is working the 11.50 ex Grosmont.

⬧ One of two Southern Railway locomotives on the North Yorkshire Moors Railway, Class S15 No. 841 "Greene King" is a 1927 design improvement of a London & South Western Railway mixed traffic locomotive. Built in 1936, it was withdrawn from service in 1964. After 8 years in Barry scrapyard, it was purchased by the Essex Locomotive Society in 1972 and restored on the Stour Valley Railway - being named at that time. Moved first to the Nene Valley Railway, then to the North Yorkshire Moors Railway in 1978. Seen here leaving Grosmont tunnel with the 13.50 for Pickering.

The third visiting main line locomotive on the North Yorkshire Moors Railway is the ever popular ex LMS "Jubilee" class No. 5690 "Leander" which spent part of the summer of 1983 on the railway. The train here is the 12.55 ex Grosmont, climbing the 1 in 49 gradient at Beckhole.

⚫ Ex BR Class J72 No. 69023 "Joem" and RSH 0-6-0ST No. 62 power their way up through Beckhole with a heavy service train. Though 69023 was built in 1951 for BR, the first of the class was built as long ago as 1898 for the North Eastern Railway.

⬙ The Tanfield Railway, just south of Gateshead, is the oldest railway in the world, first having opened in 1725. It is home to some 30 industrial locomotives and some fascinating stock. These three pictures show two of their engines - RSH 0-4-0ST "Sir Cecil A. Cochrane" and 0-6-0ST "Progress" - working the line.

◐ Most preserved railways these days try to provide added interest on their Gala days by running exhibition freight trains. On the North Yorkshire Moors Railway, ex LMS Class 5 No 45428 "Eric Treacy" - named after the famous railway photographer - is seen with a train at Green End Wood. There were 842 Class 5 locomotives built for the LMS. No. 45428 was bought in October 1967 when it was withdrawn from service and has been on the railway since 1973

◐ The latest locomotive to be restored at the Great Central Railway is ex LMS Class 8F No. 48305 - rescued from Barry scrapyard after a 7 year stay. It is seen approaching Rothley sidings hauling a rake of restored open mineral wagons.

⬆ **Ex LMS Class 3F No. 47279 recreates the classic branch line "pick up" freight train at Ingrow on the Keighley and Worth Valley Railway.**

◀ **On the Severn Valley Railway, ex LMS Class 8F No.8233 leaves Highley with a mixed freight train. During World War 2, this locomotive worked for 3 years in Persia and thereafter in the Suez Canal Zone before returning to England and British Rail in 1952.**

▶ **(Over) In May 1984 a summer steam passenger service from Fort William to Mallaig was started. Ex NBR and LNER Class J36 No. 673 "Maud" was an unlikely participant, but is seen here struggling up to Glenfinnan station. The engine was built in 1891 and was one of 25 of it's class shipped to France during World War 1 and named on their return.**

⬣ Perhaps the most eagerly awaited event since the end of steam on the main line in 1968 was the inaugural run of ex LMS "Coronation" class No. 46229 "Duchess of Hamilton", seen here leaving York station on the 10th May 1980 with the "Limited Edition"

⬣ Ex LNER Class A4 No. 4498 "Sir Nigel Gresley" in it's LNER and BR days hauled all the famous streamlined and other expresses between King's Cross, Yorkshire and Scotland. In preservation it has been a regular performer on the main line. The locomotive is working a Marylebone to Stratford on Avon excursion train at Bucknell just north of Bicester.

⬧ 70000 "Britannia" was the first locomotive to be built to British Railways own design in 1951, the class extending to 55 locomotives. Withdrawn in 1966, it was stored till 1971 when it went to the Severn Valley Railway. After extensive restoration at Carnforth the locomotive returned to the main line in 1991, seen here at Ais Gill summit on its maiden trip over the Settle-Carlisle line.

⬧ The Bulleid Pacifics when introduced in 1941 to the Southern Railway had several innovative features including chain driven valve gear. All the Merchant Navy class were rebuilt in the late 1950s. 35005 "Canadian Pacific" is seen in it's final form crossing Swithland viaduct on the Great Central Railway.

◭ Ex LMS "Jubilee" class No. 5690 "Leander" bursts out of Baron Wood Tunnel with a southbound "Cumbrian Mountain Express"

◖ (Opposite top) Ex LMS "Jubilee" class No. 45596 "Bahamas" heads south at Smardale with a "Cumbrian Mountain Express". The locomotive was built in Glasgow in 1935 and was withdrawn from service in 1966. Apart from 45742, it is unique in it's class in having had a double chimney fitted in May 1961.

◖ (Opposite bottom) Ex LMS No. 44767 "George Stephenson" was one of 842 "Black Five" mixed traffic locomotives, but was unique in being fitted with roller bearings, double chimney and Stephenson link valve gear. It is seen here working the luxury "Royal Scotsman" train between Fort William and Mallaig.

◁ (Opposite top) 1986 was another red letter year for Railway Preservation when No. 4468 "Mallard" - the holder of the World Speed Record of 126 mph - was restored to main line running condition. The A4 is seen here at Strensall en route from it's home base at York to Scarborough with the "Mallard 88"

◁ (Opposite bottom) The Gresley designed V2s were equally at home on fast freight trains and top link express passenger trains. Based at York in the National railway Museum, No. 4771 "Green Arrow" crosses Ais Gill viaduct with a southbound "Cumbrian Mountain Express"

◁ Arguably the most famous preserved locomotive in the world is ex LNER Class A3 No. 4472 "Flying Scotsman". Built in Doncaster in 1923, it hauled the first non-stop train from King's Cross to Edinburgh on 1st May 1928. It is seen here on the Carnforth-Skipton leg of a north bound "Cumbrian Mountain Express"

⬤ After 10 1/2 years in Barry scrapyard following withdrawal from British Rail in 1962, and a further 16 years of restoration work at the Buckinghamshire Railway Centre, ex GWR "King" class No. 6024 "King Edward 1" returned to steam in May 1989. In April 1990 the locomotive is seen heading a "Shakespeare Express" at Wood End tunnel.

⬤ Though built for British Rail in 1950, No. 7029 "Clun Castle" came from a distinguished lineage of GWR four cylinder 4-6-0 locomotives. Purchased privately following withdrawal in 1965 to form the basis of the Tyseley Museum, the locomotive was a regular performer on the main line after the steam ban was lifted. Seen here leaving it's birthplace at Swindon with an excursion train for Gloucester.

⏶ Described as the "Flagship of the Fleet", No. 6000 "George V" was built in 1927 and almost immediately went to the USA on tour. Withdrawn from service in 1962, the locomotive was preserved as part of the National Collection. After restoration by Bulmers Ltd. of Hereford the engine was very active in the early years of preservation. Seen here at Severn Tunnel Junction on a train from Hereford to Swindon.

⏶ Ex GWR "Castle" class No. 5080 "Defiant" was built in 1939 and withdrawn from service in 1963. After a spell in Barry scrapyard it was bought by the Birmingham Railway Museum as a source of spare parts for 7029 "Clun Castle". Happily, however, the locomotive was eventually restored to main line running and is seen here on a "Shakespeare Express" leaving Wood End tunnel en route for Stratford-on-Avon.

⬥ In the annals of Railway Preservation some strange double-heading occurred. Such a pairing was on the EMI Express charter train from Edinburgh to Gleneagles, with ex LNER No. 4771 "Green Arrow" and ex BR No. 92220 "Evening Star" seen at Blackford.

⬥ Early morning back lighting catches ex LMS "Black 5" No. 5305 as it approaches Banavie en route from Fort William to Mallaig.

⬭ On this occasion the late afternoon back lighting highlights ex MR "Compound" 4-4-0 No. 1000 and ex LMS "Jubilee" class No.5690 "Leander" as they storm through Horsforth en route from Leeds to York.

⬭ Ex SR "King Arthur" Class N15 No. 30777 "Sir Lamiel" was built in Glasgow in 1925 and worked virtually all it's life out of Waterloo. It was withdrawn from Basingstoke shed in 1961 and after a long period in store was moved to Humberside Locomotive Preservation Group for restoration, making it's main line debut on 27th March 1982. It is seen here on the Great Central Railway with a service train from Leicester North.

⬥ One of the classic Railway Centres, and the hub of many of the preserved main line steam specials, was York station. Ex LMS "Coronation" class No. 46229 "Duchess of Hamilton" is seen leaving the north end of the station with a special for Leeds

⬥ The classic shot of the south end of York station shows ex SR "Merchant Navy" class No. 35028 "Clan Line" leaving with a special for Carlisle.

⬥ The grandeur of the architecture of York station can be seen as ex BR No. 92220 "Evening Star" arrives in the centre platform with a special from Leeds to Scarborough.

⬆ Ex LNER Class A3 No. 4472 "Flying Scotsman" approaches Stratford-on-Avon with the "Half Century Limited" - a private charter train run from London Marylebone to celebrate the 50th birthday of the owner of the locomotive - Sir William McAlpine.

▶ (Opposite top) The magnificence of the Settle-Carlisle line is well seen as ex LNER No. 4472 "Flying Scotsman" crosses Smardale viaduct with a northbound "Cumbrian Mountain Pullman".

▶ (Opposite bottom) With bright winter back lighting, ex LNER No. 4472 "Flying Scotsman" heads up the Hope Valley away from Cowburn tunnel with a Guide Bridge to York train.

◭ Early morning winter sun catches ex LNER No. 4472 "Flying Scotsman" at Whittlesey as it travels from March shed to Peterborough.

◄ (Previous page) The 1 in 49 average gradient from Grosmont to Goathland is a severe test for any locomotive, as can be seen when ex WD No. 3672 "Dame Vera Lynn" approaches Goathland at Darnholme.

► (Top) Ex SR No. 850 "Lord Nelson" is caught by a shaft of light out of an otherwise threatening sky as the train - a northbound "Cumbrian Mountain Express" - crosses Ribblehead viaduct.

► (Bottom) Ex LMS class 5 No 5305 skirts Loch Eil on it's return trip from Mallaig to Fort William with the "West Highlander". This locomotive was withdrawn from service in 1968 and sent for scrapping to Mr A.E.Draper at Hull. Happily it was preserved and, after restoration by the Humberside Locomotive Preservation Group, returned to the main line in 1976.

🔼 **Ex GWR "Castle" class No. 5051 "Drysllwyn Castle"** approaches Fenny Compton as the sun sets with the return trip from Stratford-on-Avon to Didcot with the Great Western Society's preserved rake of GWR coaches. 5051 was built in 1936 and was withdrawn from service in 1963. After 7 years in Barry scrapyard, it was restored at Didcot - returning to the main line in 1980.

◀ *(Previous page - left)* **The inaugural main line run of ex SR "West Country" class No. 34092 "City of Wells"** took place on one of the coldest December days ever known. The train is at Kettlesbeck Bridge en route from Carnforth to Skipton.

◀ *(Previous page - right)* **Ex LMS Class 5 No 5305** reaches Ais Gill summit in glorious winter sunshine with a southbound "Cumbrian Mountain Express". Mr A.E.Draper, who died in 1977, rescued 5305 for preservation when it was sent to his yard for scrapping. As a mark of respect, the locomotive was named after him in 1984.

▶ *(Opposite top)* **The warm glow of the setting December sun** catches ex GWR No.3440 "City of Truro" at Haxby as it heads from York to Scarborough. This locomotive is famous for being the first steam locomotive to haul a train on the main line in excess of 100mph - a feat carried out on 9th May 1904.

▶ *(Opposite bottom)* **As ex LMS Class 8F No. 48151 accelerates** away from Appleby en route for Carlisle, the last rays of the setting sun catch the locomotive and train.

⬣ Silhouettes of locomotives at sunset are notoriously difficult. The arrival of the locomotive has to coincide with the maximum glow in the sky - and can never be pre-arranged. Here ex BR Class B1 No. 1306 "Mayflower" times the approach to Quorn on the Great Central Railway exactly as the November sun is setting.

⬣ Ex LMS "Jubilee" class No. 45593 "Kolhapur" was withdrawn from Leeds Holbrook shed in 1967 and was purchased for preservation at Tyseley. After restoration, 45593 returned to the main line in 1985, though it has been on the Great Central Railway for the last 3 years. Seen here leaving Quorn en route for Loughborough at sunset.